ACROSS A SHEET OF PAPER

ACROSS A SHEET OF PAPER

A selection of poems translated from the German

CHRISTINE MCNEILL

All rights reserved. No part of this work covered by the copyright herein may be reproduced or used in any means – graphic, electronic, or mechanical, including copying, recording, taping, or information storage and retrieval systems – without written permission of the publisher.

Printed by imprintdigital
Upton Pyne, Exeter
www.digital.imprint.co.uk

Typesetting and cover design by The Book Typesetters
us@thebooktypesetters.com
07422 598 168
www.thebooktypesetters.com

Published by Shoestring Press
19 Devonshire Avenue, Beeston, Nottingham, NG9 1BS
(0115) 925 1827
www.shoestringpress.co.uk

First published 2022
© Copyright: Christine McNeill
© Cover photograph: Christine McNeill

The moral right of the author has been asserted.

ISBN 978-1-915553-00-3

ACKNOWLEDGEMENTS

Acknowledgements are due to the following magazines in which some of the translations first appeared: *Acumen*, *Cyphers*, *Dream Catcher*, *Stand Magazine*.

I would like to thank my husband, David King, for his invaluable comments and suggestions.

CONTENTS

Introduction   1

POET AND POEM

Silent Poem   5
   Hugo Salus (1866–1929)
Poems   6
   Julian Schutting (1937)
I Fear the Words People Say   8
   Rainer Maria Rilke (1875–1926)
Old Poem   9
   Heiner Müller (1929–1995)
The Poet   10
   Jakob Haringer (1898–1948)
Entry   11
   Rainer Maria Rilke (1875–1926)
Intermezzo   12
   Alois Hergouth (1925–2002)
Across A Sheet of Paper with Poems   13
   Heiner Müller (1929–1995)
Language   14
   Elisabeth Borchers (1926–2013)
Only Two Things   15
   Gottfried Benn (1886–1956)
He Who Is Alone   16
   Gottfried Benn (1886–1956)
Unchained   17
   Stefan Zweig (1881–1942)
Speaking Softly in Small Crises   18
   Elfriede Gerstl (1932–2009)
Mother Tongue   19
   Christine Busta (1915–1987)

THE CHILD

Each evening I ask… 23
Ingeborg Bachmann (1926–1973)
For A Child 24
Günter Bruno Fuchs (1928–1977)
Childhood 25
Rainer Maria Rilke (1875–1926)
Dream Wood 27
Heiner Müller (1929–1995)
In Front of the Mirror 28
Mascha Kaléko (1907–1975)
What Shall I Call Myself 29
Ingeborg Bachmann (1926–1973)
On the Beach 30
Marie Luise Kaschnitz (1901–1974)
Crossing 31
Hilde Domin (1909–2006)
To A Child 32
Elisabeth Borchers (1926–2013)
Verse to A Boy's Found Objects 33
Christine Busta (1915–1987)
Keep Still 34
Mascha Kaléko (1907–1975)

SOUL AND SPIRIT

Song of the Spirits Above the Waters 37
Johann Wolfgang von Goethe (1749–1832)
Silence 39
Eva Strittmatter (1930–2011)
We Three 40
Else Lasker-Schüler (1869–1945)
Yearning 41
Alois Hergouth (1925–2002)
Love Song 42
Rainer Maria Rilke (1875–1926)

Harmony	43
Georg Trakl (1887–1914)	
Gaze into A River	44
Nikolaus Lenau (1802–1850)	
Angel Songs	45
Rainer Maria Rilke (1875–1926)	
My Mother	46
Else Lasker-Schüler (1869–1945)	
Evening Sensations	47
Friedrich Hebbel (1813–1863)	
A Dream	48
Johann Gottfried Herder (1744–1803)	
When in infinity…	49
Johann Wolfgang von Goethe (1749–1832)	
What Do You Need	50
Elfriede Mayröcker (1924–2021)	
Fresh Snow	51
Christian Morgenstern (1871–1914)	
The Golden Rope	52
Hilde Domin (1909–2006)	
Time Stands Still	53
Mascha Kaléko (1907–1975)	
In that life takes…	54
Rainer Maria Rilke (1875–1926)	
A Lot of Courage	55
Marie Luise Kaschnitz (1901–1974)	
New Land	56
Hilde Domin (1909–2006)	
Passing Landscape	57
Hilde Domin (1909–2006)	
The Question	58
Stefan Zweig (1881–1942)	

SPRING

Early Spring	61
Max Dauthendey (1867–1918)	
The First Lark	62
Arno Holz (1863–1929)	
Spring	64
Rose Ausländer (1901–1988)	
Swallow and Fly	65
Friedrich Hebbel (1813–1863)	
Gifts of the Wind	66
Hilde Domin (1909–2006)	
Snowfall	67
Franz Werfel (1890–1945)	
Above Your Flowerbed	68
Doris Mühringer (1920–2009)	
The Woods Are Silent	69
Erich Kästner (1899–1974)	
The Cockerel	70
Christine Busta (1915–1987)	
Easter Saturday Legend	71
Bertolt Brecht (1898–1956)	
Resurrection	72
Marie Luise Kaschnitz (1901–1974)	
Time and Again	73
Rainer Maria Rilke (1875–1926)	
The Pond	74
Annette von Droste-Hülshoff (1797–1848)	
It has been raining abundantly…	75
Christine Lavant (1915–1973)	
Beginning	76
Eva Strittmatter (1930–2011)	
Return III	78
Rose Ausländer (1901–1988)	
Caller for Help	79
Hilde Domin (1909–2006)	

REFLECTIONS ON AGEING AND THE FINAL JOURNEY

On Ageing   83
Christine Busta (1915–1987)
About the Ivy   84
Peter Härtling (1933–2017)
Blue Hydrangea   85
Rainer Maria Rilke (1875–1926)
Dream Boats   86
Jeannie Ebner (1918–2004)
Nocturnal Secret   87
Friedrich Nietzsche (1844–1900)
What Will Be Left of Me   88
Eva Strittmatter (1930–2011)
Butterfly   89
Nelly Sachs (1891–1970)
Like A Wave   90
Hermann Hesse (1877–1962)
Poppy   91
Alois Vogel (1922–2005)
World   92
Nelly Sachs (1891–1970)
Sinking Sky   93
Stefan Zweig (1881–1942)
Chorus of the Saved Ones   94
Nelly Sachs (1891–1970)
I Am the Night   96
Selma Meerbaum-Eisinger (1924–1942)
Memento   97
Mascha Kaléko (1907–1975)
My Old Violin   98
Anton Wildgans (1881–1932)
Music   99
Rainer Maria Rilke (1875–1926)
Corona   100
Paul Celan (1920–1970)
The Unsteady Scales of Life   101
Rainer Maria Rilke (1875–1926)

Old Man on the Island of Fire	102
Armin T. Wegner (1886–1978)	
Light	103
Eva Strittmatter (1930–2011)	
Things	104
Friedl Hofbauer (1924–2014)	
The Way You Should Be Kissed	105
Erich Fried (1921–1988)	
I Only Know	106
Rose Ausländer (1901–1988)	
Unceasing	107
Jeannie Ebner (1918–2004)	
On the Edge	108
Christine Busta (1915–1987)	
You Are Still Here	109
Rose Ausländer (1901–1988)	
Authors' Biographical Notes	111
Copyrights	118

INTRODUCTION

This book grew over a number of years as I was attracted to particular poems, first by having heard them recited and the spoken word making a strong impression on my mind, and secondly studying them on the page, entering the poem's context and structure, and searching to find a close equivalent in English.

Once I had accumulated a sizeable collection, I began to order the poems into themes that appealed to me and that I wanted to explore. *What does it mean to be a poet? How does a poem come about?* From these questions the first section emerged: POET AND POEM. Others followed organically as I began to see a link (sometimes in a word or image) between the last poem of each section and the first one of the next.

So it happened that THE CHILD – focusing on the search for identity, the meaning of language, as well as the memory of childhood and parental care – followed. SOUL AND SPIRIT developed from Mascha Kaléko's poem "Keep still" that ends the previous section.

I wanted to include a section about nature, and SPRING seemed the most obvious choice for its thrust into light, and yet often shadowed by the dark, both in natural and human terms.

The fifth section, REFLECTIONS ON AGEING AND THE FINAL JOURNEY, appears perhaps strange, succeeding as it does SPRING, but here I was led by Hilde Domin's line "In me there is always a farewell" at the beginning of the final poem in SPRING. For this part, I selected poems that not only conveyed the process of reflection, but also of survival.

The poets are taken from different periods; some will be familiar, others not. As for my translation, I would rest my case with Julian Schutting's definition: "… every poem / is a translation of a poem / only existing in translations / a poem is what declares itself to be a poem."

Christine McNeill

Poet and Poem

SILENT POEM

There is a kind of silent poem
That neither invents nor reports,
That, as with slim, pale, soft
Fingers, strokes across your forehead
And dreamily opens the door of your soul
Like a gentle flow of air;
Glides through your soul
Breathing words in passing
That suddenly move you to tears.

Hugo Salus (1866–1929)

POEMS

A poem is something amid a white plain,
fenced in and enclosed
in the cups of its lines;
it has forgotten where and how it became,
but it isn't a lost bird
for it mirrors, by merely mirroring itself,
also the mood from which it emerged;
a poem is a window
opening into a strange reality
behind which only the one of a poem is visible,
or a wall with blind windows,
or the moment before a butterfly
crumbles to dust,
a painted seal,
a script of signs and images
made of contradicting images and signs,
a sea-shell without the murmur of the sea,
the ghost-hour of an object,
an apple on a winter's tree,
but not a rose disabled by frost,
something that reminds of something
of which there is no recollection,
the final image in a row of images
diminishing into infinity,
a sign for something
for which only in poems there are signs,
an imitation of something not even dreamt of,
something speaking to itself in hidden sources,
playing at moving them somewhere else,
chaining moon phases to one another
and weighing down words with landscapes,
an island of language,
a reflection in a blind mirror,
something connecting the literalness of words
in such a way that meanings emerge from the link-up,
a forged banknote,

an astrological sign
that does not agree with its name,
a door in the middle of a meadow,
a piece of wallpaper in a burnt-out house,
a game of football as a pretext for players
to assemble colours and lines,
the difference between a real
and a drawn dove,
a pure presence,
every poem is a cup
around a possibly burned kernel,
every poem is a translation
of a poem
only existing in translations,
a poem is what declares itself to be a poem.

Julian Schutting (1937)

I FEAR THE WORDS PEOPLE SAY

I fear so much the words people say.
They define everything so precisely:
this is called *dog* and that *house*,
here is the beginning, and there is the end.
I'm scared too of their meaning, their playful mockery.
They know everything, what will be and what was,
for them no mountain holds any wonder;
their garden and home border straight on God.
I always want to warn and resist: Stay away –
I enjoy hearing things sing!
You touch them: they are numb and mute.
To me, you kill every thing.

Rainer Maria Rilke (1875–1926)

OLD POEM

At night, swimming across the lake,
There is a moment that puts you in question.
There are no other moments any more.
At last the truth
That you're only a quote
From a book you haven't written.
Against that you can always write
On your fading typewriter ribbon –
The text shines through.

Heiner Müller (1929–1995)

THE POET

All the happiness was never bliss,
And the most dazzling star never turns into light.
Also the most profound misery on earth
Was never just suffering: it turns into a poem.
Life's most beautiful things are
Only verses, and to your heart mere gewgaws.
Every poet is a blind child.
Words are his poor fatherland.
He solely seeks the rhyme in all life.
Oh, rhyme for him spoils his being –
He never found hand nor home.
He is only a poet who endlessly dies.
A poet who never prayed,
Walking like a corpse through life.
To him the world is a dead city
For he only has his own heart to live in.

Jakob Haringer (1898–1948)

ENTRY

Whoever you may be: leave your room
in the evening in which you know everything;
the last object before the horizon is your house,
whoever you may be.
With tired eyes that can hardly free
themselves from the well-worn threshold,
you slowly lift a black tree
and place it before the sky: slender, alone.
And you have made the world. It is large
and like a word still maturing in the silence.
As your will comprehends its meaning,
your eyes tenderly let go of it ...

Rainer Maria Rilke (1875–1926)

INTERMEZZO

Sometimes one should risk it,
get up and walk away.
Away from the books
and question marks,
from the spiralling smoke
that blurs the window.
To be alone, without memories.
Not write the poem
sounding in one's ear.
Keep it secret,
or tell it to the flowers and trees,
to the birds in the blue that sing and sing
as if it were really so beautiful.

Alois Hergouth (1925–2002)

ACROSS A SHEET OF PAPER WITH POEMS

Across a sheet of paper with poems
Fresh from the typewriter
Runs an insect.
I can't say if it would have been fun,
But I know full well:
I would have killed it ten years ago without hesitation.
What has changed – I, or the world?

Heiner Müller (1929–1995)

LANGUAGE

Are you the issue that we invoke?
Are you the lit steps leading down into a poem?
Are you what is above and what is below?
The middle ground you do not recognise.
Are you the flight, the fall,
and no one gets up any more,
and what you ask finds no response.
And what you know belongs nowhere.

Elisabeth Borchers (1926–2013)

ONLY TWO THINGS

Gone through so many forms,
through I and We and You,
yet all still sustained
by the eternal question: What for?

That is a child's question.
Very late you realised
there is only one thing: to endure –
whether sense, obsession, saga
is not determined by you: You just have to.

Whether roses, snow, or seas,
all that flowered, withered;
there are only two things: emptiness
and the scarred self.

Gottfried Benn (1886–1956)

HE WHO IS ALONE

He who is alone is also in the secret,
he always stands in the flood of images,
in their conception, their germination,
even shadows carry their embers.

He is heavy with each and every layer,
his intellect fulfilled and conserved,
powerful in the destruction of all
that is human and feeds and breeds.

Without emotion he sees how the earth
became different from when he began,
no longer *Dying* or *Becoming:*
with form arrested, completion looks him in the face.

Gottfried Benn (1886–1956)

UNCHAINED

The circle of things in which you are woven
Only impoverishes you when it completely overwhelms.
Only when you have escaped its approaching force,
Can you feel its gaze in you a hundredfold,
For from the veins of your blood emerge
Images reflecting all around;
What touches, you have long since owned.
You are every thing: blossom, tree and wind.
You are field and world, unbounded in space,
Becoming path and cloud of your creative dream;
You are a tune resting in itself,
Dreamily engrossed in your soulful silence,
And loneliness snatches from gloomy embers
Golden sparks rising to stars.

Stefan Zweig (1881–1942)

SPEAKING SOFTLY IN SMALL CRISES

I'm consistently related to myself.
At the same time drifting away from what I pursue.
I see with joy and horror
how in sentences I'm connected and replaced.
Am I the funny construct of my sentences,
and wasn't even that already somewhere in print?
Sentences come and go.
Do I really have to comprehend it all?
Am I made of language, or am I not?
A poem walking on two feet?
I do not know who is speaking here.

Elfriede Gerstl (1932–2009)

MOTHER TONGUE

Not what mother says
calms and comforts the children.
At first they don't understand it at all.

How she says it,
the tone of voice, the rhythm,
the monotony of love
in the variable sounds
opens to the senses the meaning of words,
initiates us into the mother tongue.

> Something similar
> happens also
> in a poem.

Christine Busta (1915–1987)

The Child

EACH EVENING I ASK…
(written in 1948)

Each evening I ask my mother in secret
about the ringing of the bells,
how I should find meaning in the days
and how to prepare for the nights.

Deep down I am always demanding
to tell it all completely,
to pick out chords
from the sounds around me.

Together, quietly, we listen:
once again my mother dreams me,
and, as in old songs,
she meets the major and minor of my being.

Ingeborg Bachmann (1926–1973)

FOR A CHILD

I have prayed. Take some sun and go.
The trees will be green.
I have told the blossoms to adorn you.

If you come to the river, there waits a ferryman.
At night his heart sounds across the water.
His boat has golden timbers; it will carry you.

The shores will be inhabited.
I have told the people to love you.
You will meet someone who has heeded me.

Günter Bruno Fuchs (1928–1977)

CHILDHOOD

School days pass with endless fear and time with
waiting, filled only with dull things.
Oh loneliness, oh arduous passing of time …
And then, to be let out: streets sparkle and chime,
in squares the fountains leap
and in the gardens the world grows wide.
To walk through all that in a child's dress,
quite different from others, and from those gone before:
oh wondrous time, oh passing of time,
oh loneliness.

In all that to look far out:
men and women; men, men, women
and children who are different and colourful;
here a house, and now and then a dog,
and terror soundlessly replacing trust:
oh grief without meaning, oh dream, oh horror,
oh bottomless depth.

And to play: ball and ring and hoop
in a garden which gently fades,
sometimes to brush against the grown-ups,
blindly, and feral in the haste of enthusiasm,
but in the evenings to walk quietly with small stiff
steps back home, held firmly by the hand:
oh ever disappearing apprehension,
oh fear, oh burden.

And kneeling for hours at the big grey pond
with a small sailing boat;
forgetting about it because others, similar
or more beautiful, draw their circles,

and needing to be preoccupied with one's pale
infant face that, sinking, shone out of the pond:
oh childhood, oh images slipping away.
Whither? Whither?

Rainer Maria Rilke (1875–1926)

DREAM WOOD

Tonight in my dream I walked through a wood full of horrors
Everywhere beasts with empty eyes no gaze could grasp
Between the trees carved by the frost into stone
From out of the cordon of spruce approaching through snow
Came clanking – am I dreaming or do I see what I see –
A child in full plate armour and visor
On his arm a lance whose sharp point gleamed
In the darkness of the spruce the sun consumes
Behind the dream wood beckoning to die
The last trace of day a golden line
And in the blink of an eye between stab and thrust
My face looked at me: I was that child.

Heiner Müller (1929–1995)

IN FRONT OF THE MIRROR

Where has the little girl gone with plaited hair
And blue school dress with buttons of mother-of-pearl –
On tiptoes pressing her turned up nose
Even more forcibly against the glass of the mirror
To see, as once happened to the old cook,
A distant vision of what was to come …
Oh mirror, mirror on the wall,
Where has the child been banished to?

I searched for the future in many a mirror,
But it remained to me a book with seven seals.
Now I stretch myself in the mirror of our time
And seek the past within.
But it shows me unrelentingly
The strange visage of the present,
Denying me my most inner face –
The old cook didn't mention that.

Mascha Kaléko (1907–1975)

WHAT SHALL I CALL MYSELF

Once I was a tree and bound,
then I fledged as a bird and was free,
tied up I was found in a ditch,
a dirty egg that burst, released me.

How shall I be? I have forgotten
where I come from and where I go to,
I'm possessed by many bodies,
a prickly thorn and a fleeing doe.

Today I'm friends with the maple branches,
tomorrow I rape its trunk ...
When did the cycle of guilt begin
with which I swam from seed to seed?

But inside me a beginning is still singing –
or an ending – and wards off my escape,
I want to avoid the arrow of this guilt
that seeks me in a grain of sand and in a wild duck.

Perhaps one day I can recognise myself,
a dove a rolling stone ...
Yet one word is missing! What I shall call myself,
without being in another language.

Ingeborg Bachmann (1926–1973)

ON THE BEACH

Today I saw you again on the beach,
Surf drifted toward your feet,
With your finger you dug into the sand,
Making marks, of which none remained.

Quite engrossed you were in your game
With the eternal impermanence.
A wave came, star and circle were washed away,
The wave retreated and you were ready again.

Laughingly you turned toward me,
Didn't know the pain I felt,
For the most beautiful wave pushed onto the beach
And extinguished the trace of your feet.

Marie Luise Kaschnitz (1901–1974)

CROSSING

A child
in the distance
with loose white hair
wearing a black dress
It isn't a child
it stands in a boat
turned away from me
lifts its arms
not toward me –
on the other side is land

I can only see the contours of the boat
and the for-ever known
slight
turn of the head.

Hilde Domin (1909–2006)

TO A CHILD

If we wait long enough,
then it will come.
Today, the child asks.
Today or tomorrow. A ship,
you have to know, needs time.
Vast and wide as the sea.
Then you will be grown up.
Then we can board
and make the journey.
Together. Us two.
And each in our own way.

Elisabeth Borchers (1926–2013)

VERSE TO A BOY'S FOUND OBJECTS

The bird feather from a tested wing,
a tenderly made nest of stems and moss,
and plant runes magically imprinted
in stone – happy child, whatever you may accomplish,
in this find you will possess all things
and from them can receive whatever you need:
the flight-ready and the motherly spirit,
and that final thing that fossilised hints at a plant,
preserving the essence in what had been suffered,
wholly transformed into a star on which you revolve.

Christine Busta (1915–1987)

KEEP STILL

When as a child I shared my sorrow with mother,
I can still hear what she said with a smile
I'd never seen before:
"Keep still, it will go away."

So I kept still. And some things went away.
For everything passes with time:
the great happiness, the chills and fever.
Even a day in November, no matter how grey.
Inconstancy is steadfast.

Later, when big doubts began to gnaw,
I knew full well not to complain to anyone –
for even friends misunderstand.
As often as I then lost heart,
it was that quiet voice which said:
Keep still, it will go away.

So much has already passed
like snowdrifts and gusts of wind …
And yet I've only now begun
to get gradually to the bottom of things.
The one who desires nothing cannot be robbed.
Ghosts are only there when we believe in them.
For a long, long time I haven't complained.
Suffering can't touch the one who says "It's nothing."
Be who you are. Come what may.
It will go away if you keep still.

Mascha Kaléko (1907–1975)

Soul and Spirit

SONG OF THE SPIRITS ABOVE THE WATERS

The human soul
Resembles water:
Descending from the sky
It rises skyward,
And downward once more,
Compelled to earth,
Eternally alternating.

Pouring from the high
Steep rock-face
A pure jet
Sprinkles delightfully in cloudy waves
Toward the smooth rock,
And, lightly received,
In an undulating haze
Softly rushes
Down below.

If cliffs
Stand in its way
It foams displeased
In its gradual descent
Toward the abyss.
Reaching the shallow bed
It creeps toward the grassy dale,
And in the smooth lake
All heavenly bodies
Graze their visage.

The wind is the wave's
Charming wooer;
Whipping from the ground
Surges of foam.

Human soul,
How you resemble the water!

Human fate,
How you resemble the wind!

Johann Wolfgang von Goethe (1749–1832)

SILENCE

You didn't see the silence
Behind the brow of the hill.
In this silence one must stand.
(Only stand. And not think.)
If I can wait long enough
In the cold and snow,
I may hear a word from the winds
That perhaps I'll understand.
Afterward everything will be different:
My word will be heavy with it.
It will be a trace in the new snow,
Approaching from silence.

Eva Strittmatter (1930–2011)

WE THREE

Our souls hung in morning dreams
Like sweet cherries,
Like laughing blood in trees.

Our souls were children
When they played with life.
Like the fairy tales tell it.

And of white azaleas
Sang the late summer skies
Above us in a southerly wind.

And with a kiss and a trust
Our souls were one
Like three doves.

Else Lasker-Schüler (1869–1945)

YEARNING

Know this: every fallen fruit becomes a seed,
for its yearning is always awakened by unrest
in its dead feelings: nourish them with warmth,
just as a humid summer's day
ripens the corn, making it glow.

Yearning is what we will never comprehend;
is always like spring coming and blossoming,
is like circles glowing –
and once again like falling fruit in autumn:
to make new buds grow ...
Yearning ...

For on earth there is no
quiet abiding,
only a transforming that eternally strives.
Yes, there is death: but also eternally rejuvenating release.
For on earth one must yearn.

Alois Hergouth (1925–2002)

LOVE SONG

How should I keep my soul so that
it doesn't touch on yours? How should I
raise it above you to other things?
Oh I wish I could accommodate it
in darkness among something lost
in an unknown place of stillness
that doesn't oscillate with your depths.
But everything that moves you and me
binds us together like the stroke of a bow
drawing *one* voice from two strings.
On which instrument are we stretched?
And which violinist has us in his hand?
Oh sweet song.

Rainer Maria Rilke (1875–1926)

HARMONY

The brightest sounds in the thin air
Sing of today's distant mourning,
A day so filled with unimagined fragrances,
A day making us dream of never experienced thrills.

Like prayers for lost companions
And quiet echoes of pleasures sunk into the night,
Leaves fall in long abandoned gardens
Which bask in the silence of paradise.

In the bright reflections on pure water
We see the death of time strangely return to life,
And our passions, bleeding,
Lift our souls to distant heavens.

We go through death reborn
To deeper torments and delights;
In this the unknown godhead acts –
And infinite new suns complete us.

Georg Trakl (1887–1914)

GAZE INTO A RIVER

If you saw happiness gone by,
Never to be found again,
It's good to gaze into a river
Where everything swells and recedes.

Oh! Stare into it long and deep,
You will find it easier not to miss
The loved one
Who was taken from your heart.

Look down unblinkingly into the river
Till tears drop from your eyes
And watch them warmly gush
Into the flood below.

In dreams, oblivion will
Close the heart's wound;
The soul with all its sorrows
Will watch itself flow past.

Nikolaus Lenau (1802–1850)

ANGEL SONGS

For a long time I did not let my angel go,
and he became depleted in my arms,
grew small, and I grew tall:
all at once I was mercy
and he a mere quivering plea.

So I gave him his heavens
and he left me with what was near, whence he disappeared.
He learned how to glide, and I to thrive,
and slowly we recognised one another ...

Since my angel no longer keeps watch over me
he is free to unfold his wings
and pierce the stillness of stars,
for he must no more hold anxious hands
over my lonely night –
since my angel no longer keeps watch over me.

Rainer Maria Rilke (1875–1926)

MY MOTHER

Was she the tall angel
That walked beside me?

Or does my mother lie buried
Underneath a sky of smoke –
It never blooms blue over her death.

If only my eyes were shining brightly
And brought light to her.

If my smile were not sunken into my face,
I would hang it above her grave.

But I know a star
On which it is always day:
I shall carry it across her earth.

Now I shall be forever alone
Like the tall angel
That walked beside me.

Else Lasker-Schüler (1869–1945)

EVENING SENSATIONS

Amicably day and night
Struggle with one another.
How to temper,
How to resolve that?

Pain, that oppressed me,
Are you already asleep?
What was it that made me happy –
Tell me, my heart!

Joy, and sorrow too,
I feel have faded,
And softly,
Slumber came in their place.

Floating away
Steadily upward,
Life seems to me
As whole as a lullaby.

Friedrich Hebbel (1813–1863)

A DREAM
(first verse of 'Amor and Psyche on a tombstone')

A dream, a dream is our life
Here on earth.
Like shadows on waves
We float and fade
And measure our sluggish steps
In space and time;
And are (not knowing it) amid
Eternity.

Johann Gottfried Herder (1744–1803)

WHEN IN INFINITY…

When in infinity, the same thing
That repeats itself, flows eternally,
When the thousandfold vaulted heaven
Closes in on its mighty self,
Then love of life streams out of every thing,
From the smallest to the largest star,
And every urgency, every struggle
Finds eternal peace in God, the Lord.

Johann Wolfgang von Goethe (1749–1832)

WHAT DO YOU NEED

what do you need? a tree a house
to measure how big how small the human life
how big how small when you look up to the crown
and lose yourself in green luxuriance
how big how small you consider how short
your life if compared with the life of trees
you need a tree you need a house
not for you alone only a corner a roof
to sit to think to sleep to dream
to write to keep silent to see a friend
the stars the grass the flower the sky

Elfriede Mayröcker (1924–2021)

FRESH SNOW

To see for the first time one's shoeprint,
a mysterious trail in fluffy snow,
to bevel a first narrow path
through the snowy field's virginal land –

such beginning is childish and delicious
when the forest murmurs round your ears
or your soul exchanges illuminated greetings
with the jagged glacier lit by the sun.

Christian Morgenstern (1871–1914)

THE GOLDEN ROPE

Nothing is as fleeting
as an encounter.

We play like children,
invite each other and leave
as if we had time eternally.
We ache at a farewell,
gather tears like marbles
and try out the knives.
Already a name is called.
Already the recreation is over.

We hold fast
to the golden rope
and resist setting out.
But it breaks.
We drift:
away from the same town,
away from the same world,
underneath the same
all-enveloping
earth.

Hilde Domin (1909–2006)

TIME STANDS STILL

Time stands still. We are the ones passing.
And yet, when on a train we are wafted along,
House, field and grazing cattle
Speed past us like phantoms.
Someone waves, and vanishes as in a dream,
Along with house and field, with lamp post and tree.

Thus too the landscape of our life streams
Past us to a different star
And is already distant on its approach.
We try in vain to make it stop,
Knowing full well that everything is only a deception.

While our train covers the allotted distance,
The landscape remains.

Time stands still. It is we who speed on.

Mascha Kaléko (1907–1975)

IN THAT LIFE TAKES…

In that life takes and gives and takes again
we are made from giving and taking:
fluctuating, transforming, ghost-like,
and yet in our soul so determined

to survive this upheaval;
trusting, upright, unflinching,
driven from day into night, from night into day
from which life emerges unceasingly

from our life, blood from our blood,
zest from our zest; pain that we accept
and from which at once we separate
because our lonely soul already deigns

to move on …

Rainer Maria Rilke (1875–1926)

A LOT OF COURAGE

I do find there is a lot of courage in the world,
If one thinks of days when it doesn't really get light.
And the years quite without hope. If one thinks
That there's no one without problems,
At the very least: Child, what will happen to you?
And we all know how much we mistrust
The roof over our heads and the earth under our feet.
And that none of us wants to say any more:
Rose, brother and sister, death,
Home, eternity.

And yet, today I saw someone
Planting a beech tree, a thin stem,
And looking up as if its crown were already curving above.
The whole day I saw lorries loaded with planks and doorsteps,
With beams and red bricks,
I saw my own face in the mirror when I left to meet you.
How joyful it was.

Marie Luise Kaschnitz (1901–1974)

NEW LAND

It was easy to be like new land
when the day came
and not to ask
and to send one's voice into the blue
like a lark.
And to get up again after falling
without scars.

The earth has turned once too often.
It didn't help
that the old woman
tied three blades of grass round my foot
as if I were a sick foal.
I got up
with scars.

If you want to wait
till I am as I was,
you must wait for me to die.
The dead, one says, have a smooth face
and fulfill our every wish.
They are cheerful
like the sky in spring.

And without asking,
without being hurt,
they are always
the kernel,
never the husk.

Hilde Domin (1909–2006)

PASSING LANDSCAPE

One must be able to walk away
and yet be like a tree:
rooted in the ground,
standing fast while the landscape passes.
One must hold one's breath
till the wind eases
and the unfamiliar air begins to encircle us,
till the play of light and shade
from green to blue
shows the old pattern
and we are at home
wherever that may be
and are able to sit down and lean
as if on the gravestone
of our mother.

Hilde Domin (1909–2006)

THE QUESTION

The evening, bleeding into night,
Always touches your soul with the same question,
For daily with the dying day you float
Into the dark that floods the world.

You're caught in the silent circle,
A flickering light in the cold spheres of stars,
And, listening out from a confusing dream,
You can only apprehend the approaching flood of unnamable things.

If you take a single thing from your life
And gauge it in your hollow hand,
You will feel in it a huge darkness quiver,

And every thing is like a wave to new miracles,
Already close to that final shore,
But it is the way that matters: nothing is a mere threshold.

Stefan Zweig (1881–1942)

Spring

EARLY SPRING

We paused today at the fence of a stranger's garden,
Looked, and saw the winter's grass at the pond waiting for the sun.
Withered leaves in the water as though on glass,
A clump of new violets lay on the pale bank,
And the fresh green grass lily grew by chunks of tufa.
In the sky above clouds drifted youthful in white skirts.
How much the eye is satisfied with just a little of the world!
Only for a few breaths the heart rested there,
Only a few moments did it linger ...
For we are all mere onlookers at fences
In the wide spaces of life, wishing and dreaming.

Max Dauthendey (1867–1918)

THE FIRST LARK

Between
ditches and grey hedges,
coat collar turned up,
hands in pockets,
I amble
through the early
March morning.

Fallow grass,
iridescent puddles and black wasteland
as far as I can see.

Among them,
leading into the centre of the horizon,
as if frozen,
a row of willows.

I pause.
No sound. Nowhere a sign of life.
Only the air and the land.

And sunless
as the sky
I feel
my heart.

Suddenly – a sound!

A timid, tender, trembling cheering,
which slowly
rises
higher and higher!

I look up at the clouds.

Above me,
whirling, plummeting, fluttering, turning,
blissfully winged, scarcely seen,
a black spot,
dashing
through
ever brighter streaming light
the
first lark!

Arno Holz (1863–1929)

SPRING

With the scent of acacia
spring flies into your
astonishment

Time says
I am a thousandfold green
and bloom in many colours

The sun calls laughingly
I give you again for free
warmth and splendour

I am the breath of the earth
the air whispers

The scented lilac
makes us young

Rose Ausländer (1901–1988)

SWALLOW AND FLY

On the brightest morning the most cheerful swallow
Fell from the sky, landing dead at my feet.
At midday, looking at the already rigid open beak,
I noticed a fly in its throat, which the bird
Had only half swallowed. It wriggled still,
I pulled it out, and, drying its wings in a ray of sun,
It soon buzzed off.

Friedrich Hebbel (1813–1863)

GIFTS OF THE WIND

The air an archipelago
of fragrant islands.
Wafts of lime blossom
and hay touched by the sun,
sweetly familiar,
stand waiting for me,
as if wrapped in cloth
woven long ago
by my mother
in a kindly home.

I am as in a dream, scarcely
believing the gifts of the wind.
Clouds of tenderness
catch me,
and happiness sinks
its small tooth
into my heart.

Hilde Domin (1909–2006)

SNOWFALL

Oh such slow falling of snow,
An endless veiling drift!
Were my eye yet steeled to the mind,
It would not remain unaware
That each flake of this white wind
Is willed, weighed, and counted.

Oh flakes, rotating in dance,
You small soul-like personalities,
Transported by gravity, lightness and wind,
In your coming and going
I see fates gliding down,
Which you begin, complete, and begin ...

One flake falls softly like wool,
Another full of obstinacy and crystal-clear,
A third rounded by resisting.
But if tomorrow this pale world dissolves,
Not one of them dies
And the purest flakes melt into drops.

Oh this slow snowfall of the world,
Such densely veiled drifting of races!
Not a single fate dies and fades.
We dissolve, but remain
When death, coming as a spring breeze,
Strikes, and gathers us as drops in its lap.

Franz Werfel (1890–1945)

ABOVE YOUR FLOWERBED

Above your flowerbed, neighbour,
above my flowerbed, neighbour,
goes the blue night.
But from your flowerbed, neighbour,
across to mine, there's no path.
Didn't the Lord consider that?

A fence runs around your house,
around my house, a tall fence,
like the large ancient trees.
Our rose-bush was pulled out.
All the roots dug out
between you and me
to build the fence.

You lie awake at night, neighbour.
I lie awake at night, neighbour.
In the giant night.
Have you thought about it, neighbour?
I have, dear neighbour.
He has considered it.

Doris Mühringer (1920–2009)

THE WOODS ARE SILENT

The seasons wander through the woods.
One doesn't notice. One reads it only in the leaves.
The seasons amble through the fields.
One counts the days. And counts the money.
One longs to escape the noisy city.

The roofs lap red-tiled waves.
The air is thick and like grey cloth.
One dreams of meadows and horses' stables.
One dreams of green ponds and trout.
And wants to visit quiet places.

One flees from offices and factories.
Where to, it doesn't matter! The Earth is round!
There, where grasses nod like familiar faces
And spiders weave silky stockings
One will be sound.

The soul is getting warped from treading concrete.
With trees one can converse as with a brother
And with them exchange one's soul.
The woods are silent. But not mute.
Whoever comes, will be consoled.

Erich Kästner (1899–1974)

THE COCKEREL

When he awoke, he saw the betrayer
bowed and whispering by the window,
and saw the henchmen walk toward their tools
to prepare for the wicked deed.

A stillness stood before the High Council ...
He saw the curtain billow at the palace,
saw the disciple turn away embarrassed,
begging wife and servant to believe:

and suddenly it grieved him to crow.

Christine Busta (1915–1987)

EASTER SATURDAY LEGEND
Dedicated to the abandoned

They took off
His crown of thorns
Lay him without dignity
Into the tomb.

When, harried and weary,
They returned to the tomb the following evening,
Behold, there sprouted a seed
From the hill of that thorn

And in the blossom, veiled in evening grey,
So quietly a thrush sang
Sweetly and gently
A bright tune.

Then, scarcely they felt death
There any more,
Saw beyond time and space,
Smiled in their bright daydream
And dreaming went their way.

Bertolt Brecht (1898–1956)

RESURRECTION

Sometimes we rise
Rise for the resurrection
In the middle of the day
With our hair alive
With our skin breathing
Only the habitual surrounds us
No mirage of palm trees
With grazing lions
And tame wolves.
The alarm clocks don't stop ticking
Their lit fingers don't extinguish.
And yet effortless,
And yet invulnerable,
Ordered in a mysterious order
Anticipated in a house of light.

Marie Luise Kaschnitz (1901–1974)

TIME AND AGAIN
(written in 1914)

Time and again, no matter whether we know the scenery of love
and the little churchyard with its lamenting names,
and the terrible concealed abyss where others
have ended: time and again we walk out in pairs
beneath the ancient trees, lie down time and again
among the flowers, facing the sky.

Rainer Maria Rilke (1875–1926)

THE POND

It lies so still in the morning light,
So tranquil, like a good conscience;
If west winds kiss its mirror,
The flowers at the edge don't feel it.
Dragonflies vibrate above,
Blue-golden and crimson tiny sticks,
And on the dazzling, sunny surface
A water spider leads a dance.
A circle of irises on the edge
Listens to the reeds' lullaby;
A mild breeze comes and goes
As if whispering: Peace! Peace! Peace!

Annette von Droste-Hülshoff (1797–1848)

IT HAS BEEN RAINING ABUNDANTLY...

It has been raining abundantly
well over nine days,
midday has no face,
only the hour strikes.
The sun perhaps has been sold
to another world
where its rays wildly fight
and its face is smashed.
The *devil's umbrellas* are open,
the *dandelions* closed,
a little meagre yellow shines
in the wild *lady's slipper*.
I ask my heart, the hour glass,
how long the world will stand,
it trembles like *quaking grass*
and has turned away.
Who is to blame for this misfortune?
I don't know the name.
Already half-drowned, but full of
patience, forget-me-nots bloom.

Christine Lavant (1915–1973)

BEGINNING

My life is made up
Of a day like today, then another.
Embers and ashes and flames.
There's nothing I bemoan.

In earlier days I felt:
Something big will happen.
Since then I have cooled down:
Small things suffice.

What big thing could come?
You get up, you lie down.
If taken apart
Everything loses its meaning.

But sometimes there are such hours
Of freedom blending into the wind.
Then I'm unleashed
And carefree like a child.

And everything is still inside me
And unhurt.
And I feel: soon it will begin,
The *miracle* is coming here and now.
What will it be? I can't say,
And yet I know: *it* doesn't exist at all.
But suddenly beyond the days
There's still a future without compulsion.

And free of fear and hope,
And thus free of time.
And all paths are open
And go a long distance.

And I can still become everything
I haven't yet been.
And between sky and earth
There is again a *beginning*.

Eva Strittmatter (1930–2011)

RETURN III

Always running away from oneself
and coming back

Celebrating the return
and denying
enduring life

Loving
people
animals and things

Loving and forgetting
and coming back
to love

Rose Ausländer (1901–1988)

CALLER FOR HELP

In me there is always a farewell:
as in the person drowning
fully clothed
heavy with seawater
giving his final love
to a small cloud.

In me there is always
belief,
as if the golden rope
whoever throws it,
is a holy redemption
for the caller for help.

Hilde Domin (1909–2006)

Reflections on Ageing and the Final Journey

ON AGEING

Love makes everything important and dear:
a shadow depression on the cheek,
the wrinkled weave around the eyes,
a childhood scar under the toes,
a concealed blemish on the skin,
a vein becoming more visible,
and the bald patch on the head.

Every loss also becomes a gain
and enriches the memory.
Tenderness is more faithful than lust,
the pain of transience renews.
Filtering gentle grief,
we rescue beauty, which abides.

Christine Busta (1915–1987)

ABOUT THE IVY

The ivy in front of the house,
I heard the gardener say at the open window,
the ivy has visibly aged.
How do you know? I asked.
And that in winter? –
Perhaps change is only apparent now
in the leafless season.
In old age, ivy doesn't climb any more
but forms small lumps,
begins – something it couldn't do before –
inconspicuously to flower.

Peter Härtling (1933–2017)

BLUE HYDRANGEA

Dull, dry and rough
like vestiges of green paint in a pot
are these leaves behind the umbels,
no longer blue, merely faintly tinged with it.

Tinged with blue, tear-stained and imprecise
as if wanting to lose it again;
and like in old blue writing paper
there is a yellow inside them, a violet and grey;

Bleached as a child's apron,
no longer worn or used:
how short-lived a small life seems.

But suddenly in an umbel the blue appears to renew itself
and one perceives it touchingly,
rejoicing in the green.

Rainer Maria Rilke (1875–1926)

DREAM BOATS

Where are they now, the silent
boats with their blue sails
passing my window
before the bright moon
in nights unfolding?

I've lived in every house,
have written my name on every threshold,
in the house of the sinner, on the door of the righteous.

But where are the black and white birds?

Islands on which dreams nest
are damaged by storm and raging sun.
Where are the boats with blue sails?
Their rotten keel turned upward,
time carries them to deserted coasts.

Where shall I build a hut?
I've lived behind every fence,
have written my name in the sand that trickled away.

Nothing is left for me.
But where are
the blue, silent, wondrous
boats of my dreams, that with a hesitant breeze
emerged from the still bays of childhood?

Jeannie Ebner (1918–2004)

NOCTURNAL SECRET

Last night, with everything asleep,
A breeze with uncertain sighs
Running through the streets,
I was given peace, not by the pillow,
Nor the poppies, nor, what at other times
Would induce deep sleep – a good conscience.
In the end I shook my senses free of sleep
And ran to the beach.
The moon was bright, the air mild – I met
A man with his boat on warm sand,
Both sleepy, shepherd and sheep.
Sleepily the boat pushed from the shore.
An hour easily, maybe two,
Or perhaps a year? – Suddenly
My senses and thoughts sank
Into an eternal All,
And an abyss opened up
Without barriers – and at once was gone!
Morning came; on dark depths
A boat stands peacefully, so peacefully –
What happened? Someone called, and a hundred
Soon followed suit – What was there? Blood?
Nothing happened! We were asleep, everyone asleep –
Oh, we slept so well, so well!

Friedrich Nietzsche (1844–1900)

WHAT WILL BE LEFT OF ME

Four sons will be left of me.
(My human alibi.)
And perhaps there will still remain a pretty
Photograph resembling me,
Which will show how I laugh.
My laughing child-face.
The face that I make when I weep
I won't show.
Then, poems will remain.
Perhaps one or two will stay
A little longer in the light than others.
Then those too will be gone.
Strange to know that
And yet to get up again.
To have to continue living
As if it would go on *forever*.

Eva Strittmatter (1930–2011)

BUTTERFLY

What a beautiful beyond
is painted in your dust.
Through the flaming core of the earth
and its strong husk
you were transported,
a soon-to-be-gone web of measured transience.

Butterfly
all creatures' good night!
The weight of life and death
sinks with your wings
down onto the rose
that withers with the homeward-bound maturing light.

What a beautiful beyond
is painted in your dust.
What royal marks
in the secrets of air.

Nelly Sachs (1891–1970)

LIKE A WAVE

Like a wave, garlanded with foam,
Rises out of the blue tide, filled with desire,
And glinting, diminishes in exhausted beauty into the large sea –

Like a cloud, sailing along in a soft breeze,
Awakens longing in every pilgrim,
And fades, pale silvery, into the day –

Like a song at the hot edge of the road,
Sounding strange with wondrous rhyme,
Moves your heart far across the land –

Thus my life flees through time,
Soon to decay, and yet will secretly arrive
In the realm of longing and eternity.

Hermann Hesse (1877–1962)

POPPY

This uncurling
in late summer
almost a gesture of humility
with bowed head
persisting and waiting again
for the next boost

The purple silken bowls
only burst when straightening up
burn in a short time
 in the fiery throat of the sky
akin to a butterfly's
velvet-soft wings
they drop to the ground

The crowned body arches
dry as paper
on the hard stem
a rattle in the autumn wind
with dark-blue dreams
toward a long winter

Alois Vogel (1922–2005)

WORLD

World, don't ask those snatched from death
where they are going,
they are always going to their graves.
The pavements of the foreign city
weren't laid for the music of refugee steps –
the windows of houses that mirror a time on earth
with their wandering displays of presents in the picture-book sky
were not honed for eyes
that had drunk the horror from its source.
The heavy iron of the world has burnt out the crease of their
 smile;
they would very much like to come to you,
but for the one without a home, all paths are withering
like cut flowers –

But, there has been a friend
in the foreign land: the evening sun.
Blessed by its tortured light
we are invited to come to it with our grief
that walks beside us:
a psalm of the night.

Nelly Sachs (1891–1970)

SINKING SKY

You, heart, that always desired the stars,
For to every wish a dream gives itself freely,
See, the sky already transfigured by evening
Lowers itself, and you scarcely believe it.

Lowers, and lowers. And earth, scared,
Lifts its face into the descending sky.
As if with deep-red lips, the spheres
Drink the final extinguishing light.

All the trees must feel it,
Steeply their pain reaches up toward evening,
And with trembling arms they bury
Themselves into the velvety floor of the stars.

The hush of distant clouds sinks,
Brushes against you like a kiss, or a dress,
Softly cradles your heart together with the stars
In close infinity.

Stefan Zweig (1881–1942)

CHORUS OF THE SAVED ONES

We, the saved ones,
From whose hollow bones death has already carved flutes,
On whose sinews death has already drawn its bow –
Our bodies still lament
With their mutilated music.
We, the saved ones,
The nooses for our necks still hang
Before us in the blue air –
The hours of the clock still fill up with our dripping blood.
We, the saved ones,
The worms of fear still feed on us.
Our star is buried in dust.
We, the saved ones,
Plead with you:
Show us slowly your sun.
Lead us at walking pace from star to star.
Let us learn quietly how to live again.
Lest the song of a bird,
The filling of a pail at the well,
Erupts our badly sealed-up pain
And washes us away –
We appeal to you:
Don't show us yet a biting dog –
It could be, it could be
That we crumble to dust –
Crumble to dust before your eyes.
What is it that holds our web together?
We, who have become breathless,
Whose soul fled out of midnight to Him
Long before our bodies were saved
In the ark of the moment.
We, the saved ones,
We press your hand,
We recognise your eyes –

But what binds us together is only a farewell,
A farewell in dust
Binds us together.

Nelly Sachs (1891–1970)

I AM THE NIGHT
(written on the 6th May 1941 in the labour-camp of Michailowka)

I am the night. My veils are
far softer than white death.
I take each hot pain with me
in my cool, black boat.
My beloved is the long road.
We are wedded for good.
I love being covered by my
silken soft black hair.
My kiss is sweet as lilac scent –
the wanderer knows it exactly …
Sinking into my arms
he forgets every hot woman.
My hands are so slender and white,
cooling every fever,
and every forehead they touch
must, against its will, softly smile.
I am the night. My veils are
far gentler than white death.
I take each hot pain with me
in my cool, black boat.

Selma Meerbaum-Eisinger (1924–1942)

MEMENTO

I'm not afraid of my own death,
only of the death of those close to me.
How shall I live when they have gone?

Alone in fog I grope along as if dead
and let myself drift docilely into the dark.
Going doesn't hurt half as much as staying.

Who has experienced the same will know it –
and those who have borne it may forgive me.
Consider: One's own death one only dies,
but that of others one has to live with.

Mascha Kaléko (1907–1975)

MY OLD VIOLIN

One day, when struggling in life
And clock and ring were pawned,
The pendant and other things,
I had to take the most painful step:
Fetched from the cabinet my old violin
To be sold.
The man looked at it critically, knocked on its wood
And finally pronounced: *It's not worth much* –
Adding with a gleeful grin:
It wasn't made by an old master.
Swallowing hard my protest and sorrow,
I took what little he was willing to part with.

Some difficult years have passed since,
But often those words come back
That so offended the old violin's tone.
A present from my parents;
Father fatigued from work and stressed,
Sat often down to a meagre meal,
Smiling at the little before him.
Mother year in year out
Wore the same new dress,
Hoping for better days.
Both saving to afford
the dear violin for their child.
Though not made by a master,
To me the violin wears a soft halo.
In its sound I always hear
What mother had endured and father suffered,
And only now I know why it pained
When that man said: *It's not worth much.*

Anton Wildgans (1881–1932)

MUSIC

For whom do I play? Oh if I knew!
I could forever murmur like a brook.

If I could divine whether dead children
like to hear the music of my inner being:

whether girls who have departed,
drift around me listening in the evening breeze.

Whether I'm softly stroking the dead hair
of someone once angry...

For what would music mean
if it could not go far beyond everything.

Surely, music, drifting on, does not know
at what point we are transformed.

That friends hear us, is all very well,
but they are not at rest

like those we can no longer see:
they feel the song of life more deeply,

for they move with what moves underneath,
and, with the final chord, they leave.

Rainer Maria Rilke (1875–1926)

CORONA

Autumn eats a leaf from my palm: we are friends.
We peel time from the nuts and teach them to go:
time returns to the husk.

In the mirror it is Sunday;
dreaming, one sleeps,
the mouth speaks what is true.

My eye lowers to the lap of my beloved:
we look at each other,
we say dark things.
We love each other like poppies and memory,
we sleep like wine in mussels,
like the sea in the blood-ray of the moon.

We stand embracing at the window, they look at us
                              from the street:
It is time that they knew!
It is time that the stone deigns to blossom,
that a heart beats to restlessness.
It is time that it is time.

It is time.

Paul Celan (1920–1970)

THE UNSTEADY SCALES OF LIFE

Unsteady scales of life
always fluctuating, how rarely
a skillful weight dares
to reveal the constantly different
load on the other side.

Beyond, the tranquil
scales of death.
Space in both the
sibling bowls.
The same amount of space. And next to it,
             unused,
all the weights of equanimity
glinting and well-ordered.

Rainer Maria Rilke (1875–1926)

OLD MAN ON THE ISLAND OF FIRE

Early morning. I open my eyes.
Behind my forehead the swallows
    Of my thoughts have gathered.
Now they're emerging from my eyes
    And are setting off.

Where are they flying to?
The sky is golden-blue above the courtyard.
I put on my trousers for walking.
Which path shall I take?

The sun sharpens its knife on the stones of the road.
I sit down on the edge of the path, and write.
Two fingers' breadth away beside my piece of paper
Eternity begins.

Armin T. Wegner (1886–1978)

LIGHT

Sometimes one meets someone who is like a light,
And one doesn't meet that person twice.
One knows: this face comes but *once*.
One thinks: it can't be
That one lost it
Before having found it,
And no *afterwards*, no *before* ...
That light is forever gone.
Secret storage, memory.
Reception and transmission centre:
In another dawn or dusk
It transforms the signals
Coming to us from that face
We only saw once,
Back into warmth and light.
It helps us to survive the night.

Eva Strittmatter (1930–2011)

THINGS

There are things more beautiful than gold and silk,
more beautiful than flowers and wind.

There are things alive only for a moment
in the sudden fright of our hearts;
a ticking clock could break or wake them.

There're things which are nothing, and yet
are the life that still stirs in what has turned to stone.

They are the sparkle in cut glass,
and the clank when it shatters.

Friedl Hofbauer (1924–2014)

THE WAY YOU SHOULD BE KISSED

When I kiss you
it isn't just your mouth
not just your navel
not just your lap
that I kiss
I kiss your questions too
and your wishes
I kiss your thoughts
your doubts
and your courage
your love for me
and your freedom from me
your foot
that came
and went away again
I kiss you
as you are
and the way you will be
tomorrow and later
and when my time has passed

Erich Fried (1921–1988)

I ONLY KNOW

You ask
what I want
I don't know

I only know
that I dream
that the dream lives me
and I float
on its cloud

I only know that I
love people
mountains gardens the sea
I only know that many dead
live inside me

I drink my
moments
I only know
it is the play of time
up and down

Rose Ausländer (1901–1988)

UNCEASING

Life keeps on happening.
It goes through me
as if I weren't there.
Does it actually see me?
No, certainly not.
But I know myself,
I cling to what I do,
my wanting, my walking and resting,
my black-on-white: my poem,
a drinking straw that the current carries along.

Am I happening? No, it happens,
and that I'm alive is perhaps
only a rumour.

Jeannie Ebner (1918–2004)

ON THE EDGE

Sometimes to sit on the doorstep,
to rest from walking, not having arrived,
the door behind you and not to knock.

To be aware of all the sounds
and not to cause one.
To receive life that is unaccepting of you:
in the house, on the street,
the heart of the mouse and of the motor,
the voices in the air and water,
people's footsteps, the stars,
the sighs of the earth and the stones.

Sometimes the light sits down beside you
and sometimes it is the shade,
faithful siblings.
Dust wants to nest on you
and untreadable snow.

Slowly under your tongue
your final word warms.

Christine Busta (1915–1987)

YOU ARE STILL HERE

Throw your fear
up in the air

Soon
your time will be up
soon
the sky will grow
under the grass
your dreams
will fall
into nowhere

Yet the carnation is still fragrant
the thrush sings

You may still love

May give away words

You're still here

Be what you are
give what you have

Rose Ausländer (1901–1988)

AUTHORS' BIOGRAPHICAL NOTES

ROSE AUSLÄNDER *(1901–1988)*: published more than 20 volumes of poetry. Growing up in a Jewish family in Bukovina, she survived the Nazi persecution in the ghetto of Czernowitz and after the end of the war lived in the USA. She wrote in German and English, and died in Düsseldorf.

INGEBORG BACHMANN *(1926–1973)*: regarded as one of the most important Austrian prose writers and poets of the 20th century, she was born in Klagenfurt, and died in a fire in her flat in Rome. As well as poetry and prose, her work also comprised essays and radio plays. She was the recipient of numerous prizes.

GOTTFRIED BENN *(1886–1956)*: German medical doctor, poet and essayist, he was an important voice in the modernist movement.

ELISABETH BORCHERS *(1926–2013)*: German author of children's books, poet, and literary translator.

BERTOLT BRECHT *(1898–1956)*: influential German dramatist, librettist and poet.

CHRISTINE BUSTA *(1915–1987)*: Austrian poet who acknowledged the work of Rilke and Georg Trakl as influences.

PAUL CELAN *(1920–1970)*: important German-speaking poet born in Romania (now the Ukraine). His work explores the possibilities of language and communication, in particular experiences relating to the holocaust.

MAX DAUTHENDEY *(1867–1918)*: German poet and artist of the impressionist movement, his work reveals a love of nature and its aesthetics.

HILDE DOMIN *(1909–2006)*: German poet of Jewish faith, translator and editor, she spent the war years in exile in the Dominican Republic. There she developed her poetic skills and took the pseudonym "Domin" in homage to that country. From 1961 until her death she lived in Heidelberg.

ANNETTE VON DROSTE-HÜLSHOFF *(1797–1848)*: prominent 19th century German poet and composer, her work combines Romanticism with Realism.

JEANNIE EBNER *(1918–2004):* Austrian prose writer and poet, mixing dreams with everyday reality, she was initially influenced by Surrealism, later by antique mythology and Christian symbolism. As editor of a literary journal, she was credited with discovering the poet Ingeborg Bachmann and other well-known writers.

ERICH FRIED *(1921–1988):* Austrian poet, translator and essayist. Born in Vienna, persecuted as Jew, he fled to London in 1938 where he lived until his death. He participated in the political discourse of his time, and in the post-war years was one of the main representatives of the "political lyric" in the German language.

GÜNTER BRUNO FUCHS *(1928–1977):* born and died in Berlin, his literary output comprised poems, short stories, novels, radio plays and children's books, which he himself illustrated.

ELFRIEDE GERSTL *(1932–2009):* Austrian poet, short story writer and essayist; as child of Jewish parents, she survived the holocaust in hiding in Vienna and later studied medicine and psychology.

JOHANN WOLFGANG VON GOETHE *(1749–1832):* German poet and naturalist, considered one of the most important exponents of German lyricism.

JAKOB HARINGER *(1898–1948):* German poet who was partially influenced by the expressionist movement.

PETER HÄRTLING *(1933–2017):* German novelist, poet, journalist and editor, who devoted a large part of his literary output to reappraising Germany's past as well as his own.

FRIEDRICH HEBBEL *(1813–1863):* German dramatist and poet, known for his love and nature lyrics.

JOHANN GOTTFRIED HERDER *(1744–1803):* German poet, translator, theologian, and philosopher of the Weimar historical and cultural classicism, he was, together with Johann Wolfgang von Goethe and Friedrich Schiller, an influential writer and thinker of the Age of Enlightenment.

ALOIS HERGOUTH *(1925–2002):* Austrian poet and translator.

HERMANN HESSE *(1877–1962):* Swiss-German novelist, poet and artist; Nobel Prize winner of literature in 1946.

FRIEDL HOFBAUER *(1924–2014):* Austrian poet, translator and writer of child and adult fiction.

ARNO HOLZ *(1863–1929):* German poet and dramatist of the impressionist and naturalist movement active in Berlin. He abandoned traditional form and rhyme in his poetry. In 1929 he was nominated for the Nobel Prize in literature.

MASCHA KALÉKO *(1907–1975):* born into a Jewish family in Galicia, she was a German poet who in 1938 fled with her family to New York. Her poems have an ironic-tender, melancholy quality, and owing to their objectivity she was often described as "the female Erich Kästner". Later poems were inspired by her life in exile. She died in Zurich.

MARIE LUISE KASCHNITZ *(1901–1974):* novelist, poet and essayist, she was born into an aristocratic family and grew up in Potsdam and Berlin. Not expressing political opinions enabled her to pursue her literary activities during the Nazi regime. She published her first poems after 1945, and received many awards, among them the prestigious Büchner Prize.

ERICH KÄSTNER *(1899–1974):* novelist, children's author, script writer, essayist and poet, he portrayed the urban society life of the Weimar republic. An opponent of the Nazi regime, he remained in Germany despite his work being declared "un-German". He was the only author present at the burning of his own books.

ELSE LASKER–SCHÜLER *(1869–1945):* was an important Jewish German poet and playwright, one of the few women affiliated with the expressionist movement. Physically harassed and threatened by the Nazis, she emigrated to Switzerland in 1933, but could not work there either. She travelled to Palestine in 1934 and finally settled in Jerusalem where she later died. Her work explores the tension between imaginary ideals and the reality of the political and her own life's circumstances.

CHRISTINE LAVANT *(1915–1973):* born the ninth child of a miner and a seamstress, she suffered poor health all her life, but nevertheless was very prolific, leaving after her death a large body of poems and stories on which her reputation as a significant Austrian writer rests.

NIKOLAUS LENAU *(1802–1850):* Austrian poet of 19th century late Romanticism. Many of his nature poems were set to music by composers such as Robert Schumann, Felix Mendelssohn-Bartholdy, Franz Liszt, and Richard Strauss.

ELFRIEDE MAYRÖCKER *(1924–2021):* born in Vienna, her avant-garde work comprises 80 poetry and prose publications, and more than 30 radio plays. Recipient of countless prizes, she described her poetry thus: "I see everything in images and penetrate them until they become language."

SELMA MEERBAUM-EISINGER *(1924–1942):* German-speaking poet of Romanian origin, she began writing poetry at fifteen years of age. Persecuted as a Jew, she died at eighteen in a labour camp in Michailowka, Romania. Her work comprises 57 poems; hand-written and bound, they were smuggled out of the camp and survived many decades in a bank safe in Jerusalem until their discovery in 1980.

CHRISTIAN MORGENSTERN *(1871–1914):* born in Munich, he was better known for his humorous verse than his so-called "serious poetry". Special features of his verse were sharp wit and word-play.

DORIS MÜHRINGER *(1920–2009):* Austrian poet, children's book author, and translator, she was a recipient of the Georg-Trakl prize.

HEINER MÜLLER *(1929–1995):* better known as a dramatist, he was also a poet, prose writer and essayist born in the former East Germany.

FRIEDRICH NIETZSCHE *(1844–1900):* German philosopher, cultural critic, composer, poet, philologist, and classical scholar whose work has exerted a profound influence on Western philosophy and modern intellectual history.

RAINER MARIA RILKE *(1875–1926):* born in Prague, he died in Valmont, Switzerland, and wrote in German and French. His work comprised not only verse, but stories, a novel, essays on art and culture, translations, as well as extensive correspondences that formed an important part of his literary output. He was an intensely accurate poetic observer of the outer and his own inner world.

NELLY SACHS *(1891–1970):* German-Swedish poet and prose writer of Jewish descent who was spared a Nazi concentration camp by being granted a visa to Sweden. Her work played a major part in German-Jewish post-war literature, and she received the Nobel Prize in 1966. Through original imagery and many-layered meanings, she found a creative way to confront annihilation and loss.

HUGO SALUS *(1866–1929):* published numerous volumes of poetry and short stories, and was one of the more important exponents of German-Jewish literature of the Prague of his day. A friend and mentor of Rainer Maria Rilke, his verse had some influence on Rilke's early lyric style. Salus made use of Jewish folktales and observances in his poetry, plays and fiction.

JULIAN SCHUTTING *(1937):* Austrian prose writer and poet who has published several volumes of poetry. His interest lies in a discourse between philosophy and language.

EVA STRITTMATTER *(1930–2011):* German poet and prose writer, known for her quiet and precise reflections on nature and the world.

GEORG TRAKL *(1887–1914):* Austrian poet born in Salzburg, where he lived for the first twenty-one years of his life, his work displays expressionist and symbolist influences, though it cannot be fully ascribed to any particular movement. It is controversial how much his reliance on drugs affected the form and content of his verse. Suffering from acute depression he died of a cocaine overdose at a military hospital in Kraków.

ARMIN T. WEGNER *(1886–1978):* German poet and pacifist, he wrote expressionist verse and countless travelogues. He lived on the island of Stromboli and in Rome.

FRANZ WERFEL *(1890–1945)*: Austrian writer of Jewish German-Bohemian descent, he went into exile to the USA and in 1941 became a US-citizen. He died there in 1945. In the 1920s and 30s his books were bestsellers. His popularity rested on his novels and stage plays, though he himself rated his poetry far more.

ANTON WILDGANS *(1881–1932)*: Austrian poet and dramatist who was nominated for the Nobel Prize in 1932 but died beforehand. Known for his socially critical works, he was also for a time director of the Vienna Burgtheater. His literary style was described as moderate expressionist. One of his sons became a musician and composer.

ALOIS VOGEL *(1922–2005)*: Austrian prose writer and poet whose work reflects life in Austria in the 1920s and 30s, in particular that of his own youth in working-class districts of Vienna.

STEFAN ZWEIG *(1881–1942)*: born in Vienna, he died in exile in Brazil during World War II, and is chiefly known for his prose, though poetry was very important to him. Strongly influenced by Rilke and Hugo von Hofmannsthal, his verse tends toward symbolism and is melancholy in tone. During his lifetime he was the most frequently read German author and many of his works belong to the canon of world literature.

COPYRIGHTS

Rose Ausländer © S. Fischer Verlag, Frankfurt am Main

Ingeborg Bachmann © Piper Verlag, Munich

Gottfried Benn © Klett-Cotta, Stuttgart

Elisabeth Borchers © Suhrkamp Verlag, Frankfurt am Main

Bertolt Brecht © Bertolt-Brecht-Erben / Suhrkamp Verlag

Christine Busta © Otto Müller Verlag, Salzburg

Paul Celan © Suhrkamp / Insel Verlag

Hilde Domin © S. Fischer Verlag, Frankfurt am Main

Jeannie Ebner © merbod Verlag, Wiener Neustadt

Erich Fried ©Verlag Klaus Wagenbach, Berlin

Günter Bruno Fuchs © Insel Verlag

Elfriede Gerstl © Literaturverlag Droschl, Graz / Vienna

Peter Härtling © Kiepenheuer & Witsch Verlag

Alois Hergouth © Styria Verlag, Graz

Hermann Hesse © Suhrkamp Verlag, Frankfurt am Main

Friedl Hofbauer © Bergland Verlag, Vienna

Mascha Kaléko © dtv Verlagsgesellschaft mbH & Co. KG

Marie-Luise Kaschnitz © Insel Verlag, Frankfurt am Main

Erich Kästner © Atrium Verlag AG, Zurich + Thomas Kästner

Christine Lavant © Wallstein Verlag, Göttingen

Elfriede Mayröcker © Suhrkamp Verlag, Frankfurt am Main

Doris Mühringer © Vierviertelverlag, Strasshof, Vienna

Heiner Müller © Suhrkamp Verlag, Frankfurt am Main / Berlin

Nelly Sachs © Suhrkamp Verlag, Berlin

Julian Schutting © Autor, Residenz Verlag, Vienna

Eva Strittmatter © Aufbau Verlag GmbH & Co. KG, Berlin

Armin T. Wegner © Peter Hammer Verlag, Wuppertal

Alois Vogel © Hanser Verlag, Munich